# The Mud Pie Party

by Jill McDougall

illustrated by Marko Rop

**OXFORD**
UNIVERSITY PRESS
AUSTRALIA & NEW ZEALAND

Rhino liked to play tricks on his friends. He pulled Monkey's tail and blew bubbles in Frog's face. Sometimes he made Hippo jump.

One day, Rhino saw his friends under a tree. They were looking at a card. Rhino crept up behind Hippo and shouted ...

## ... "Boo!"

Hippo jumped in the air and the card
fell out of her hand.

The card said:

Come to a Mud Pie Party
at the swamp this afternoon.

"Yippee!" cried Rhino. "I love making
mud pies. See you at the party!"

That afternoon, Rhino ran to the party. On the way, he met a little tiger.

"Are you going to the party?" asked Rhino.

"No," said the little tiger. "Hippo told me that someone who plays mean tricks is going."

"You can come to the party with me," said Rhino. "I'll make sure no one plays any mean tricks."

At the party, Rhino stood on a log. "Someone here plays mean tricks," said Rhino. "We must find them and stop them."

"Yes!" said Monkey. "He pulls my tail."

"He blows bubbles in my face," said Frog.

"He creeps up behind me," said Hippo. "And he shouts ... **Boo!**"

Rhino got such a fright that he fell off the log.

"Now I know who has been playing mean tricks," cried Rhino. "It's **me!**"

"I'm sorry," said Rhino. "I won't play mean tricks again."

After that, everyone had fun at the party.

No one pulled Monkey's tail. No one blew bubbles in Frog's face and no one made Hippo jump.

But everyone made lots and lots of ...

... mud pies!

# Retell the Story

1

2

3

Come to a Mud Pie Party at the swamp this afternoon.

4

5

6

7

8